Word Fun

PICTURE WINDOW BOOKS
Minneapolis, Minnesota

Fun

If you were ...

a noun, a verb, an adjective, an adverb, a pronoun, a conjuntion, an interjection, a preposition

written by Michael Dahl and Nancy Loewen

illustrated by Sara Gray

PICTURE WINDOW BOOKS
Minneapolis, Minnesota

Editor: Christianne Jones
Designers: Hilary Wacholz and Tracy Davies
Page Production: Melissa Kes
Art Director: Nathan Gassman
The illustrations in this book were created with acrylics.

Picture Window Books
151 Good Counsel Drive
P.O. Box 669
Mankato, MN 56002-0669
877-845-8392
www.picturewindowbooks.com

Printed in China

 All books published by Picture Window Books
are manufactured with paper containing at
least 10 percent post-consumer waste.

Library of Congress Cataloging-in-Publication Data
Dahl, Michael.
A noun, a verb, an adjective, an adverb, a pronoun, a
conjunction, an interjection, a preposition / written by
Michael Dahl and Nancy Loewen ; illustrated by Sara Gray.
p. cm. — (Word fun)
ISBN 978-1-4048-4426-1 (paperback)
1. English language—Parts of speech—Juvenile literature.
2. English language—Grammar—Juvenile literature.
I. Loewen, Nancy, 1964- II. Gray, Sara, ill. III. Title.
PE1199.D34 2008
428.2—dc22   2008013432

Table

Special thanks to our advisers for their expertise:
Rosemary G. Palmer, Ph.D., Department of Literacy
College of Education, Boise State

Terry Flaherty, Ph.D., Professor of English
Minnesota State University, Mankato

# of Contents

noun **(n.)** a word that names a person, place, or thing

If

You were a noun...

... you would be

a STAR,

a CLOUD,

8

an ASTRONAUT, or the MOON. Let's blast off into the world of nouns!

If you were a noun, you would be easy to spot. You would be a person, a place, or a thing.

You could be an
ASTRONAUT

preparing to fly into SPACE in a **SPACESHIP.**

If you were a noun, you could be proper. A proper noun is a specific person, place, or thing. The first letter of a proper noun is always capitalized.

A rocket flies out of Cape Canaveral in Florida.

Names are proper nouns, so they are always capitalized.

The first astronaut to walk on the moon was **Neil Armstrong.**

13

If you were a noun, you could be a single thing. A noun that is one thing is a singular noun.

14

You could be one ALIEN with one EYE and one TENTACLE.

If you were a noun, you could be more than one thing. A noun that is more than one thing is a plural noun. Some nouns change from singular to plural by adding an "s" to the end.

16

You could be many ALIENS with many EYES and many TENTACLES.

17

If you were a noun, you might change your shape. Some singular nouns have to change their shape when they become plural nouns.

GALAXY becomes GALAXIES.

MOUSE becomes MICE.

WOMAN becomes WOMEN.

If you were a noun, you might look the same whether you were a singular or a plural noun.

one **FISH**

two **FISH**

seven **FISH**

How many fish do you see?

If you were a noun, you might have more than one way to describe yourself. Some things have more than one plural noun to describe them.

Clouds of space gas and dust are **NEBULAS** or **NEBULAE**.

Small, cool stars are **RED DWARFS** or **RED DWARVES.**

If you were a noun, you could be a group or a collection of things. You would be a collective noun.

You could be a **CREW** of astronauts,

You could be a **CONSTELLATION** of stars,

a SWARM of meteors,

or a COLONY of space pioneers.

25

You could grow, expand, and never stop. You could become an infinity of universes ...

... if you were a noun!

The NOUN GAME

This is a guessing game to be played with a group of people.

Directions: Have each person think of a noun. Next, have each person pick three words to describe the noun. For example, if a person picked an "ice cube," he or she would say, "I am frozen, hard, and slick." Take turns guessing each person's noun.

Fact: If you look up a noun in the dictionary, you will see the letter "n" next to it. The "n" stands for noun.

verb (v or vb) a word that is used to express an action or condition

If you were a verb... 29

... you could SWIM,

DANCE,

TIPTOE,

LEAP,

PADDLE,

CARTWHEEL,

TRAVEL,

or PLUNGE.

31

Verbs get things going!

If you were a verb, you could BALANCE and BEND, TWIST and TURN,

SWOOP and SOAR.

33

If you were a verb, you would appear in every sentence.

You would be in every book, every newspaper, every magazine, and every letter ever written.

35

If you were a verb,
you could be an action.

The mighty ship
SAILS out of the harbor.

Waves **CRASH** against its side.
Seagulls **SCREAM** overhead.

If you were a verb, extra words would help you show action. These extra words are called helping verbs.

You **MAY** give the usher your ticket now.

POPACORN

The popcorn **WILL BE** popping soon.

The movie **HAS** started on the big screen.

If you were a helping verb, you would have 23 members in your family: may, might, must, be, being, been, am, are, is, was, were, do, does, did, should, could, would, have, had, has, will, can, shall.

If you were a verb, you could link things together. You would be a linking verb. Sometimes linking verbs are called state-of-being verbs.

The swimmer **WAS** tired.

6

The beach ball **IS** floating.

The lifeguards **WERE** done for the day.

If you were a linking verb, your most common forms would be is, am, were, was, are, be, being, and been.

If you were a verb, you would change when time passed. You could be in past tense, present tense, or future tense.

Last night, the bicycles GLIDED through the park.

Now, the bicycles **GLIDE** through the park.

Tomorrow, the bicycles **WILL GLIDE** through the park.

If you were a verb, you would change when the number of people or things change.

One acrobat **SWINGS** above the crowd,

but five acrobats *SWING* above the crowd.

If you were a verb, you would get together with other verbs to make cool and exciting sentences.

The rocket SPEEDS toward the space station

46

that **WHIRLS** and **SPINS** above Earth.

You could always be moving ...
... if you were a **verb!**

FUN with VERBS

Verbs can be full of action. Verbs can also be quiet.

Directions: Think of an action verb, such as running, jumping, or flying. Then make your friends guess what the verb is by acting it out. See how quickly they can figure out what your secret verb is. Take turns acting out action verbs and guessing.

Next, choose a quiet verb, such as standing, sleeping, thinking, staring, wishing, or hiding. Take turns acting out quiet verbs and guessing.

Is it harder to act out an action verb or a quiet verb?

Fact: If you look up a verb in the dictionary, you will see the abbreviation "v" or "vb" next to it. The "v" or "vb" stands for verb.

adjective (adj)

a word that describes or modifies
a noun or pronoun

If you were an

adjective...

... you
would be

COLORFUL!

BRILLIANT!

DAZZLING!

FEATHERY!

MANY-LEGGED!

SHIMY!

53

If you were an adjective, you would work side by side with nouns. A noun names a person, place, or thing. As an adjective, you would be busy describing nouns.

An elephant is a noun.

If you were an adjective, you would tell us about the elephant.

The **GRAY** elephant is **GIGANTIC** and **WET**.
The **SPARKLING** water cools down the **HOT** elephant.

If you were an adjective, you would tell us how a person, place, or thing looks.

The **SLENDER** swimmer snaps a photo of

the **ENORMOUS** whale in the DEEP, BLUE water.

If you were an adjective,
you would describe things.

The TINY kittens are FLUFFY.

The LITTLE piglets are PUDGY and PINK.

The COLORFUL peacock's tail is BIG and BRIGHT.

59

If you were an adjective, you would describe how something sounds.

The howler monkey is **LOUD!**

60

The boa's movement is SILENT.

The **QUIET** mouse
watches and waits.

61

If you were an adjective, you would describe how something feels.

The alligator's back is RIDGED and BUMPY.

If you were an adjective, you would describe how something behaves.

The **FEARLESS** plover is **CAREFUL** when it picks at the alligator's teeth.

If you were an adjective, you might be a proper adjective. A proper adjective describes a specific object and is always capitalized.

In winter, the **Arctic** fox's coat turns white to blend in with the snow of the **Alaskan** tundra.

67

If you were an adjective, you could compare things. You would change your ending to show how things are different.

You would be a comparative adjective if you compared two things.

The turtle is **SMALL.**

The tree frog is **SMALLER.**

You would be a superlative adjective if you compared three things.

The lion is **FAST.**

Yes!

The antelope is **FASTER.**

The swift is the **FASTEST** of the three.

You could be BAD,

WORSE, WORST, or

GOOD,

BETTER. BEST ...

... if you were an adjective.

Fun with Adjectives

Directions: Write your name from top to bottom on a piece of paper. Now, think of adjectives that describe you. Use the letters in your name as the first letters of the adjectives. For example, you might write:

Mysterious
Intelligent
Creative
Happy
Athletic
Easy-going
Loud

Then, see if you can find adjectives to describe your friends.

Fact: If you look up an adjective in the dictionary, you will see the abbreviation "adj" next to it. The "adj" stands for adjective.

71

adverb (adv) a word that describes or modifies a verb, an adjective, or another adverb

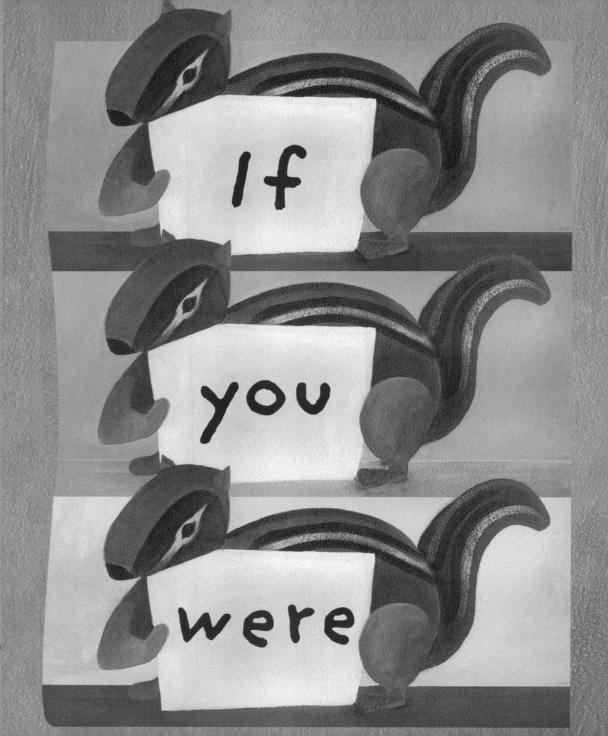

73

SLOPPILY,

LOUDLY,

or ENERGETICALLY!

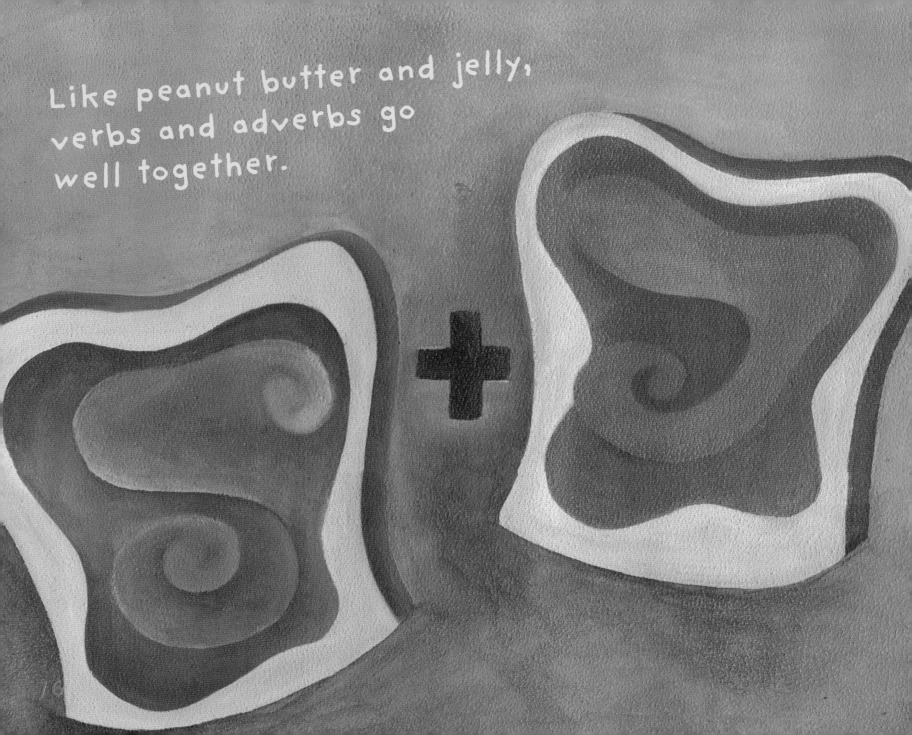

Like peanut butter and jelly, verbs and adverbs go well together.

If you were an adverb, you would work closely with verbs.

Verbs tell us something happened. If you were an adverb, you could tell us how something happened.

The snowboarder skied GRACEFULLY down the mountainside,

but he fell **AWKWARDLY**
at the bottom.

If you were an adverb, you might have a tail. Many adverbs end in the letters "ly."

How did the bear dive?

CLUMSILY

PERFECTLY

SPEEDILY

The volleyball player hit the ball SHARPLY and POWERFULLY. A player on the other side jumped FEARLESSLY into the air.

81

If you were an adverb, you would work at the beginning, the middle, or the end of a sentence.

RAPIDLY, the runner rounded the curve.

The runner **RAPIDLY** rounded the curve.

The runner rounded the curve **RAPIDLY**.

If you were an adverb, you could tell us how often something happens.

The long jumper **ALWAYS** jumps

The long jumper **OFTEN** jumps

more than 20 feet (6 meters).

more than 28 feet (8.5 meters).

If you were an adverb, you could tell us when something is going to happen. You could be something NOW, LATER, TODAY, TOMORROW, or YESTERDAY.

Some teams will play NOW.

Other teams will play **LATER**.

If you were an adverb,
you could help adjectives
describe things better.

Some athletes are
SOMEWHAT short.

Some athletes are **VERY** tall.

Some athletes are **IMMENSELY** muscular.

Some athletes are **EXTRAORDINARILY** fast.

Some athletes are **TOO** busy practicing.

If you were an adverb,
you could modify
other adverbs.

The crowd watches **VERY CLOSELY** as the athletes

compete **EXTREMELY** **WELL**.

You would put together
super sentences ...

... if you were
an adverb!

The ADVERB GAME

Directions: Choose someone to be "it," and have that person go out of the room. Have the rest of the group choose an adverb.

Call your friend back into the room. Have your friend pick someone in the group to act out the adverb. For example, "Walk across the room like the adverb."

Your friend must watch for clues and then guess what the adverb is. Do they move swiftly or dreamily or spookily?

Your friend can pick up to three different people to act out the adverb in different ways. After three chances, explain what the adverb was, choose another person from the group to be "it," and start over.

Fact: If you look up an adverb in the dictionary, you will see the abbreviation "adv" next to it. The "adv" stands for adverb.

pronoun (pron) a word that takes the place of a noun

If you were
a pronoun...

... **YOU** could throw a party.
YOU would invite

HIM and **HER** and **THEM** and **US**.

YOU would invite **EVERYBODY!**

"Come **ONE**, come **ALL**," **YOU** would say. "**WE** will have a terrific time!"

If you were a pronoun, you would replace nouns and take the repetition out of sentences.

Without Pronouns

Jessie put Jessie's backpack in Jessie's locker. Then Jessie went to talk to Jessie's friends.

With Pronouns

Jessie put **HER** backpack in **HER** locker. Then **SHE** went to talk to **HER** friends.

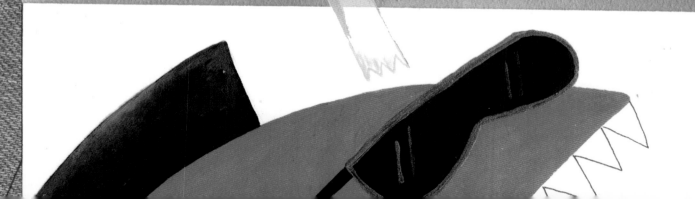

If you were a pronoun, you could take the place of more than one person or thing.

Carol, Bruce, and I earned a pizza party for the entire class.

WE earned a pizza party for the entire class.

Frank and Dylan each ate three slices of pizza. THEY each ate three slices of pizza.

If you were a pronoun, you could take the place of a person or a person's name. You would be a personal pronoun.

Mrs. Jones handed out the tests.

SHE handed out the tests.

Brian was nervous for the test.

HE was nervous for the test.

If you were a pronoun, you could be possessive. You would let people know that something belongs to someone or something.

Sharky lost some of **HIS** teeth.

OUR playground equipment needs to be cleaned.

If you were a pronoun, you could tell about people and things without being specific. You would be an indefinite pronoun.

Did I forget **SOMETHING?**

EVERYONE get ready to march.

I don't want to trip over **ANYTHING**.

SOMEBODY lost some sheet music.

Other common indefinite pronouns include SOMEONE, ALL, ANYONE, NO ONE, ANY, EVERYBODY, NONE, SEVERAL, SOME, BOTH, NEITHER, NOBODY, NOTHING, and MANY.

If you were a pronoun, you could ask questions.
You would be an interrogative pronoun.

WHAT is in here?

WHO understands this stuff?

WHICH is the right one?

WHOM and WHOSE are other interrogative pronouns.

If you were a pronoun, you could point something out without naming it. You would be a demonstrative pronoun.

Please give me **THOSE.**

I'll take **THESE.**

If you were a pronoun, you could be like a mirror. You could reflect the subject of the sentence back to itself. The subject tells whom or what the sentence is about.

I can fix it MYSELF.

THEY will get THEMSELVES into a lot of trouble if THEY eat THEIR textbooks!

If you were a pronoun, you could emphasize the subject of the sentence.

The principal **HERSELF** decorated the set for the school play.

You would always
be working hard
as a stand-in ...

... if you were
a pronoun!

Fun with Pronouns

Gather some friends and some old newspaper or magazine articles.

Give each player a highlighter or a bright crayon.

When someone says go, quickly read through your articles, marking every pronoun you see.

Try doing this for one minute. After one minute, the player with the most pronouns wins.

Fact: If you look up a pronoun in the dictionary, you will see the abbreviation "pron" next to it. The "pron" stands for pronoun.

conjunction (conj) a word that

joins together other words or groups of words

If you were a

conjunction...

OR salty AND bitter.

119

If you were a conjunction, you would be a connector. You would be the rope that ties ideas together.

I'll take the barbecued burger on a sesame seed bun

with a tomato **AND** lettuce,

BUT I don't want onions on the burger **UNLESS** they're fried.

If you were a conjunction, you could join single words or groups of words. You would be called a coordinating conjunction. You would be a word with two or three letters.

The brownies were warm **AND** gooey,

YET the milk was cold

AND refreshing.

The waiter served two pails of ice cream,

BUT it wasn't enough for our party.

The cake was gone, **SO** the monkey ordered banana bread instead.

Common coordinating conjunctions include and, but, or, nor, for, so, yet.

If you were a coordinating conjunction, you could turn two sentences into one.

Zach drank a big carton of milk.
He burped loudly.

Zach drank a big carton of milk, **AND** he burped loudly.

If you were a conjunction, you might work with a partner. You would be called a correlative conjunction. You and your partner would always work together.

PICK ME

PICK ME

EITHER a strawberry **OR** a pineapple would be fine.

Common correlative conjunction pairs include both/and, either/or, neither/nor, not only/but also, so/as, whether/or.

126

He wanted **NOT ONLY** mustard and ketchup,
BUT ALSO relish for his corn dog.

RELISH

MUS-

If you were a conjunction, you could join two clauses. You would be called a subordinating conjunction.

I couldn't buy another treat **BECAUSE** I spent all of my money.

128

Since it was cold out, she bought a cup of hot soup.

129

If you were a subordinating conjunction, you could tell when things happen.

BEFORE

the pie-eating contest, Sally loved pie.

130

BEFORE

AFTER she won the contest, Sally vowed she'd never look at another pie again.

AFTER

If you were a subordinating conjunction, you could tell why things happen.

Edgar Elephant couldn't eat peanuts **BECAUSE** they gave him hives.

If you were a subordinating conjunction, you could tell how things happen.

Pedro gobbled down the sandwich *AS IF* he hadn't eaten in days.

You would be busy bringing things together ...

... if you were a conjunction!

Fun with Conjunctions

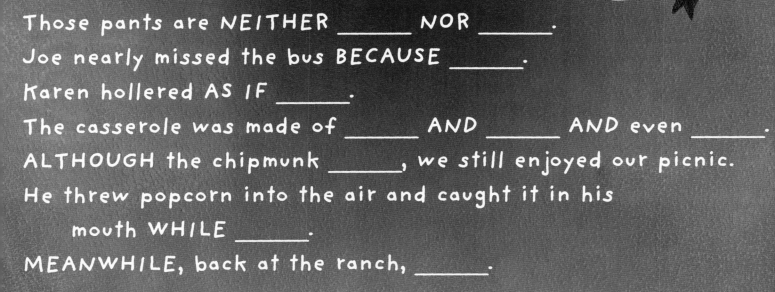

These unfinished sentences contain conjunctions. Get together with your friends and see who can come up with the craziest sentences!

Those pants are NEITHER _____ NOR _____.

Joe nearly missed the bus BECAUSE _____.

Karen hollered AS IF _____.

The casserole was made of _____ AND _____ AND even _____.

ALTHOUGH the chipmunk _____, we still enjoyed our picnic.

He threw popcorn into the air and caught it in his mouth WHILE _____.

MEANWHILE, back at the ranch, _____.

Are you done with these? Try making up your own.
Use the conjunctions in this book to get started.

Fact: If you look up a conjunction in the dictionary, you will see the abbreviation "conj" next to it. The "conj" stands for conjunction.

interjection (interj) a word or phrase that shows strong feeling or emotion

If you were an interjection...

139

... you could express a feeling.

YIPPEE!

BRAVO!

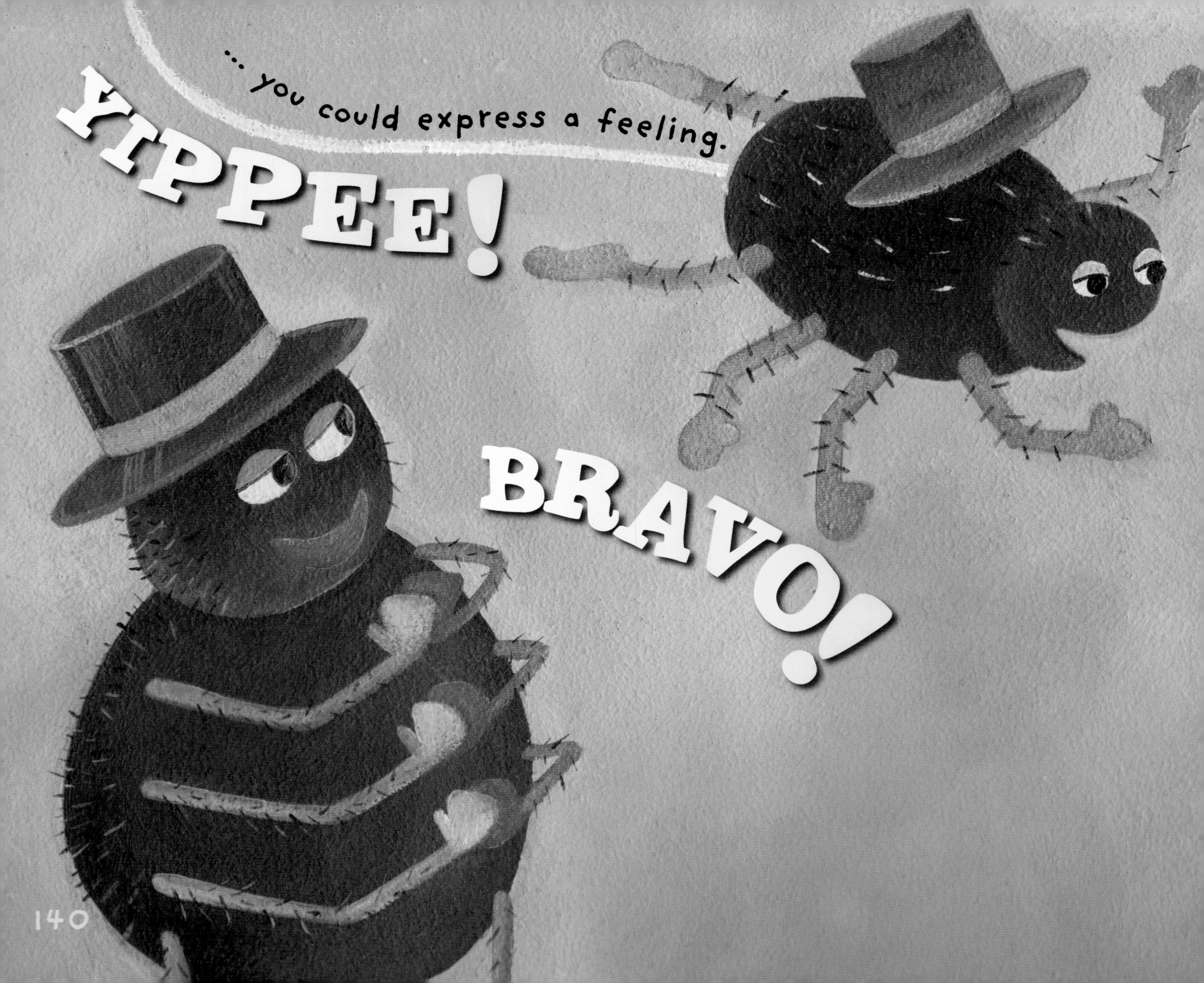

141

If you were an interjection, you would be a word or phrase that shows strong feeling or emotion.

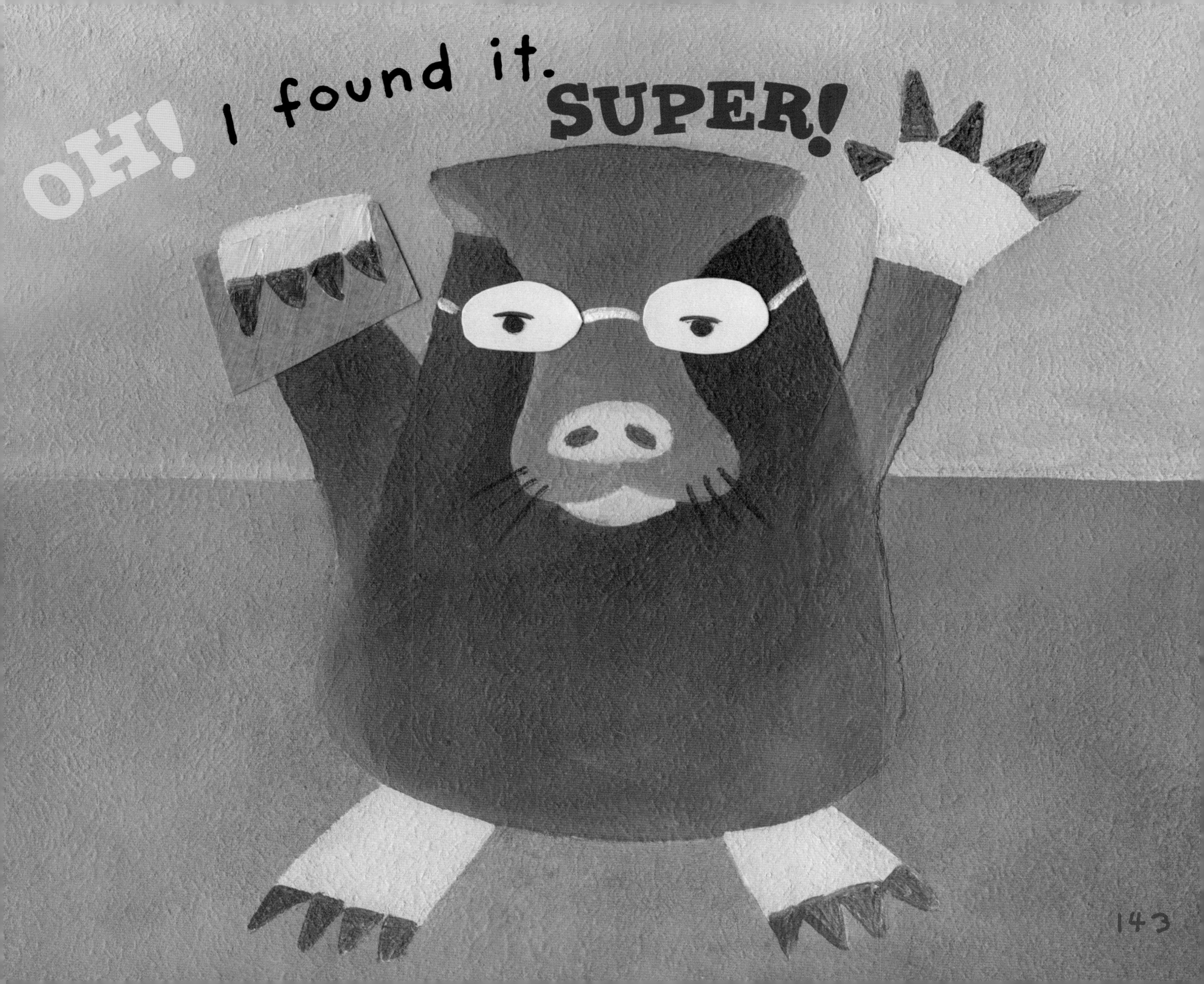
OH!
I found it.
SUPER!

If you were an interjection, you would often be used with an exclamation point.

OOPS! I didn't mean to bump into you.

OH NO!

I spilled my milk.

YIKES!

What a mess!

If you were an interjection, you could also be used with a question mark or a comma.

WELL?
Are you coming?

HUH?
What did you say?

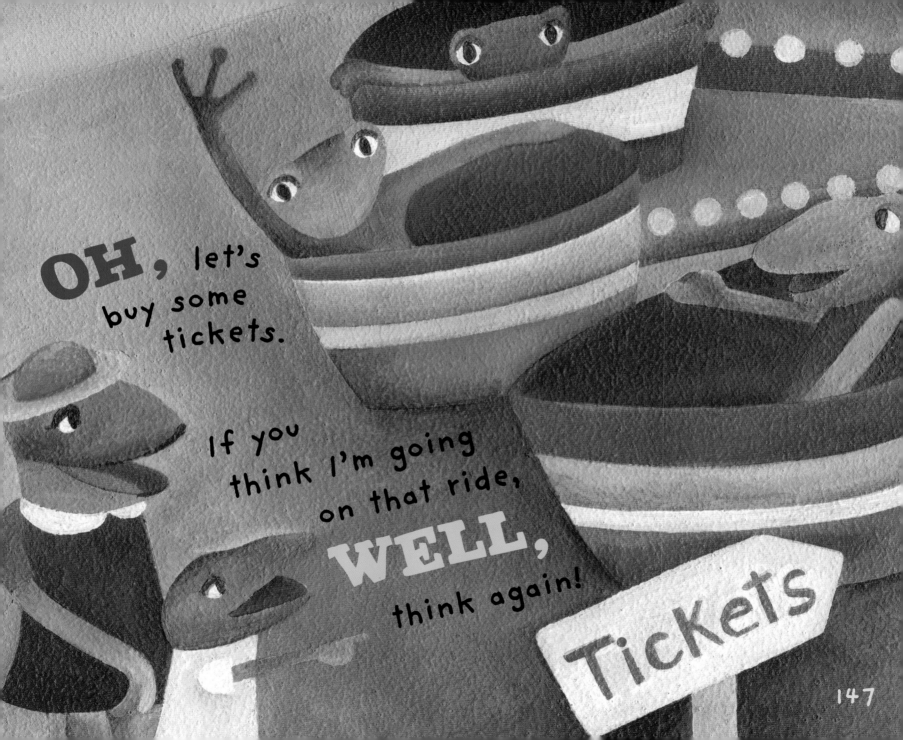

OH, let's buy some tickets.

If you think I'm going on that ride, WELL, think again!

Tickets

147

If you were an interjection, you would show feeling. You could show surprise and excitement. You could show disgust and fear.

HOORAY! Here comes the parade.

WOW, do you see how much candy the clowns are throwing at the crowd?

YUCK! I'm glad I don't have to march behind that horse.

149

If you were an interjection, you could get a
person's attention with a greeting or a farewell.

GOODBYE, Sammy!

GATE'S
Guitar
Lessons

HELLO,
Mr. Gates.

HEY, where are you?

YOO-HOO! I'm over here!

151

If you were an interjection, you could be a filler word. You would give the speaker more time to get his or her thoughts together.

UH, where did you get those note cards?

WELL ... HELLO, I seem to have lost the note cards for my speech.

That's, UM, a good question— a very good question indeed.

If you were an interjection, you could be total nonsense and still add meaning to the sentence.

OOH-LA-LA, don't you look nice!

155

OH! That's really gross!

Fun with Interjections

Interjections are often some of the funniest, most colorful words in our language. Take the word **PHEW**, for example. We use it when something doesn't smell good. Can you make up another interjection that might express the same feeling? How about **ACKMOO** or **HUFFKA**? Why not make up some of your own?

Make up interjections that could be used in the following situations:

1. When you see a big spider on the ceiling.

2. When you step on a melted ice-cream cone in the parking lot.

3. When your little sister grabs the last chocolate cupcake.

4. When your parents make leftover surprise for supper.

5. When you get into trouble for something you didn't do.

Get together with your friends and hold a contest. Have one person judge the best new interjections. Then you can all start using the winning words.

Fact: If you look up an interjection in the dictionary, you will see the abbreviation "interj" next to it. The "interj" stands for interjection.

preposition (prep) a word that shows the relation between another word and a noun or pronoun

If you were a

preposition...

circle **AROUND**

the tree,

... you could go **OUT**

and **ABOUT** the yard,

walk **ON** the fence,

slither **BETWEEN** the bushes,

or jog **BY** the snail.

If you were a preposition, you would make a sentence longer by adding more detail.

The rabbit hid **INSIDE** the hat.

I want the lizard **WITH** the red stripes.

If you were a preposition, you could tell where things are.

The goat is walking BESIDE the shed.

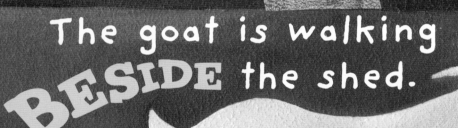

The goat
is resting
BEHIND
the shed.

Look! The goat jumped
ONTO the shed.

If you were a preposition, you could tell when things happen.

DURING the day, Hammy the hamster sleeps.

Hammy drinks his water BEFORE he works out.

168

Hammy runs on his wheel **AT** night.

If you were a preposition, you would never work alone. You would be paired with a noun or pronoun. The noun or pronoun would be your object. You and your object would form a prepositional phrase.

Tibby ate two whole cans **OF tuna!**

prepositional phrase

(preposition) (object)

All three cats sleep **WITH me.**
(prep.) (obj.)

Here, kitty!
Come **TO** me.
(prep.) (obj.)

171

If you were a preposition, you could be part of a short prepositional phrase.

prepositional phrase

ON Wednesday

(prep.)   (obj.)

prepositional phrase

TOWARD her

(prep.)   (obj.)

prepositional phrase

WITH glee

(prep.)   (obj.)

If you were a preposition, you could be part of a prepositional phrase that includes many words. These words are called modifiers. They describe people, places, things, or actions. Modifiers go between the preposition and the object of the preposition.

We saw a chipmunk **UNDER** the front step.

(prep.) (mod.) (obj.)

The dog fell asleep
BY the warm, cozy fireplace.
(prep.) (mod.) (mod.) (obj.)

If you were a preposition, you could be in a sentence with other prepositional phrases.

The tarantula crawled **FROM its cage,**

OVER the stack OF books, ACROSS the desk, and INTO the wastebasket.

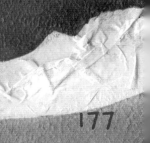

If you were a preposition, you could make a sentence more exciting. The sentence would make sense without you, but it wouldn't be nearly as much fun.

The ferret jumped.

The ferret jumped
FROM the table,
TO the lamp,
and **ONTO**
the drapes.

179

You would link words together
and add more detail ...
... if you were a preposition!

Position your Prepositions

With a group of friends, write down as many prepositions as you can. Cut the words apart, and put them in a bowl. Take turns drawing a word and acting it out. Look around for objects you can use to demonstrate the word.

For example, if you get the word "through," you could pass a coin through the slats of a kitchen chair. The first person to guess the correct answer gets a point.

Some of the prepositions will be easy to act out. Others will be difficult. You may want to give each player a hint, like what letter the preposition starts with. You could also think of a sentence using the preposition, and then say the sentence out loud without using the preposition.

Once all of the words are drawn, the person with the most points wins.

Fact: If you look up a preposition in the dictionary, you will see the abbreviation "prep" next to it. The "prep" stands for preposition.

SUMMARY

ADJECTIVE (adj) a word that describes or modifies a noun or pronoun

ADVERB (adv) a word that describes or modifies a verb, an adjective, or another adverb

CONJUNCTION (conj) a word that joins together other words or groups of words

INTERJECTION (interj) a word
or phrase that shows strong feeling or emotion

NOUN (n) a word that names a person,
place, or thing

PREPOSITION (prep) a word that shows
the relation between another word and a noun or pronoun

PRONOUN (pron) a word that takes
the place of a noun

VERB (v or vb) a word that is used to
express an action or condition

GLOSSARY

ADJECTIVE a word that describes or modifies a noun or pronoun

ADVERB a word that describes or modifies a verb, an adjective, or another adverb

CLAUSE a group of words that includes a subject and a predicate

CONJUNCTION a word that joins together other words or groups of words

COORDINATING CONJUNCTION a conjunction that has just two or three letters and connects two separate sentences

CORRELATIVE CONJUNTION a conjunction that always works with another word

DEMONSTRATIVE PRONOUN a type of pronoun that helps point something out without naming it

EMPHASIZE to give more importance to something

INDEFINITE PRONOUN a type of pronoun that tells about people and things without being specific

INTERJECTION a word or phrase that shows strong feeling or emotion

INTERROGATIVE PRONOUN a type of pronoun that asks a question

MODIFIERS words that go between the preposition and the object of the preposition and describe people, places, things, or actions

MODIFY to change in some way

NOUN a word that names a person, place, or thing

OBJECT a noun or pronoun that ends a phrase that begins with a preposition

PERSONAL PRONOUN a type of pronoun that takes the place of a person

PHRASE a group of words that expresses a thought but is not a complete sentence

POSSESSIVE PRONOUN a type of pronoun that shows that an object belongs to someone or something

PREDICATE a word or group of words that tells what the subject does or what is done to the subject

PREPOSITION a word that shows the relation between another word and a noun or pronoun

PREPOSITIONAL PHRASE a phrase that begins with a preposition and ends with an object

PRONOUN a word that takes the place of a noun

SUBJECT a word or group of words that tells whom or what the sentence is about

SUBORDINATING CONJUNCTION a conjunction that joins together two clauses to tell when, why, or how things happen

VERB a word that is used to express an action or condition

TO LEARN MORE

More Books to Read

Cleary, Brian P. *Dearly, Nearly, Insincerely: What Is an Adverb?* Minneapolis: Carolrhoda Books, 2003.

Cleary, Brian P. *Hairy, Scary, Ordinary: What Is an Adjective?* Minneapolis: Carolrhoda Books, 2000.

Cleary, Brian P. *I and You and Don't Forget Who: What Is a Pronoun?* Minneapolis: Carolrhoda Books, 2004.

Cleary, Brian P. *A Mink, a Fink, a Skating Rink: What Is a Noun?* Minneapolis: Carolrhoda Books, 1999.

Cleary, Brian P. *To Root, to Toot, to Parachute: What Is a Verb?* Minneapolis: Carolrhoda Books, 2001.

Cleary, Brian P. *Under, Over, By the Clover: What Is a Preposition?* Minneapolis: Carolrhoda Books, 2002.

Doudna, Kelly. *Adjectives.* Edina, Minn.: Abdo Pub., 2001.

Heinrichs, Ann. *Adjectives.* Chanhassen, Minn.: Child's World, 2004.

Heinrichs, Ann. *Adverbs.* Chanhassen, Minn.: Child's World, 2004.

Heinrichs, Ann. *Conjunctions.* Chanhassen, Minn.: Child's World, 2004.

Heinrichs, Ann. *Interjections.* Chanhassen, Minn.: Child's World, 2004.

Heinrichs, Ann. *Nouns.* Chanhassen, Minn.: Child's World, 2004.

Heinrichs, Ann. *Prepositions.* Chanhassen, Minn.: Child's World, 2004.

Heinrichs, Ann. *Pronouns.* Chanhassen, Minn.: Child's World, 2004.

Heller, Ruth. *Behind the Mask: A Book About Prepositions.* New York: Grosset & Dunlap, 1995.

Heller, Ruth. *Fantastic! Wow! And Unreal! A Book about Interjections and Conjunctions.* New York: Grosset & Dunlap, 1998.

Heller, Ruth. *Kites Sail High: A Book About Verbs.* New York: Grosset & Dunlap, 1988.

Heller, Ruth. *Mine, All Mine: A Book About Pronouns.* New York: Puffin Books, 1999.

Heller, Ruth. *Up, Up, and Away: A Book About Adverbs.* New York: Grosset & Dunlap, 1991.

Pulver, Robin. *Nouns and Verbs Have a Field Day.* New York: Holiday House, 2006.

Schneider, R. M. *Add It, Dip It, Fix It: A Book of Verbs.* Boston: Houghton Mifflin, 1995.

On the Web

FactHound offers a safe, fun way to find Internet sites related to topics in this book. All of the sites on FactHound have been researched by our staff.

1. Visit www.facthound.com
2. Type in this special code for age-appropriate sites: 1404844260
3. Click on the FETCH IT button.

Your trusty FactHound will fetch the best sites for you!

INDEX

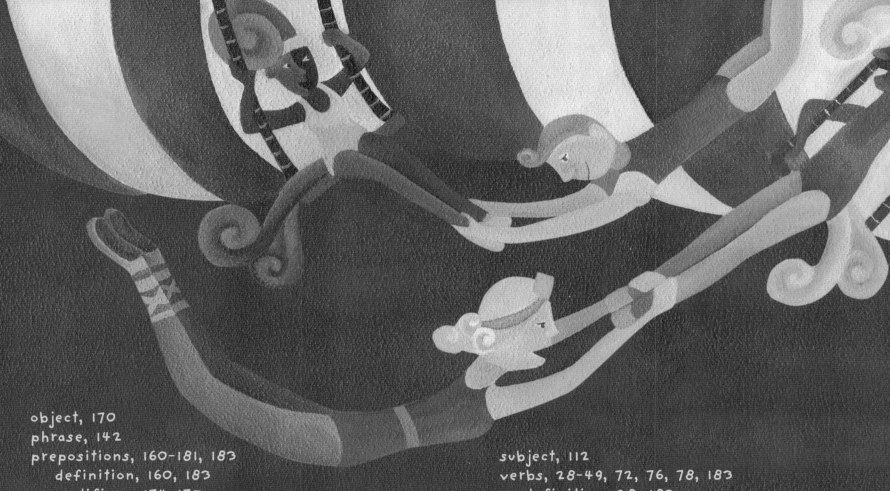

Nancy Loewen has written more than 60 children's books on a variety of topics, including insects, money, natural disasters, character development, language, and more.

Nancy's books have received awards from the American Library Association, the *New York Public Library*, and Parents' Choice. *Four to the Pole!* (Linnet Books, 2001), a young adult book co-written with polar explorer Ann Bancroft, was a Minnesota Book Award finalist.

Nancy lives in the Twin Cities with her husband, two children, and a very demanding cat. Her children hope that the cat will allow them to get a dog someday.

Sara Gray graduated with a BFA in illustration and design from the Minneapolis College of Art and Design. She has worked as a freelance illustrator for Picture Window Books, Mpls/St. Paul Magazine, and Minnesota Parent Magazine.

The Word Fun series that Sara worked on with Picture Window Books won the AEP Distinguished Achievement Award and the American Graphic Design Award.

Sara currently works at Manhattan Toy Company as a product designer for Manhattan Toy's doll, plush, and puppet lines. Her illustrations also appear on Manhattan Toy's packaging for their Cirque du Soleil product line.

Michael Dahl is the author of more than 100 books for children and young adults. He has twice won the AEP Distinguished Achievement Award for his nonfiction.

Dahl's Finnegan Zwake mystery series published by Simon & Schuster won rave reviews. Two of its titles were shortlisted for the Edgar and the Anthony mystery awards. He has also edited and written numerous graphic novels for younger readers. Michael has spoken at schools, libraries, conferences, and bookstores across the United States.

Michael currently lives in a haunted house in Minneapolis, Minnesota.